lie down too

Lesle Lewis

lie down too

Alice James Books

FARMINGTON, MAINE

10 9 8 7 6 5 4 3 2 1

Alice James Books are published by Alice James Poetry Cooperative, Inc.,
an affiliate of the University of Maine at Farmington.

ALICE JAMES BOOKS
238 MAIN STREET
FARMINGTON; ME 04938

www.alicejamesbooks.org

Library of Congress Cataloging-in-Publication Data
Lewis, Lesle.
lie down too / Lesle Lewis.
    p.   cm.
Poems.
ISBN 978-1-882295-85-2
I. Title.
PS3612.E967L54 2011
811'.6—dc22   2010044655

Alice James Books gratefully acknowledges support from individual donors,
private foundations, the University of Maine at Farmington and the
National Endowment for the Arts. ❦

Image of Alice James by permission of the Houghton Library, Harvard University.
Call number: pf MS Am 1094, Box 3 (44d)

Cover art: David Brewster, "Ruffled Grouse and Shell Bag"
   32" x 32", Oil on Mi-Tientes, 2006

For Susan, David, Stephen,

and Ron (who broke the window)

Contents

Acknowledgments I am grateful to the editors of the following journals in whose pages some of these poems first appeared, sometimes in earlier versions: *POOL, Hotel Amerika, The Cincinnati Review, jubilat, The Hollins Critic, Mississippi Review, Barrow Street, The Massachusetts Review, Bateau, Talking River, Tygerburning Literary Journal, notnostrums, Connotation Press: An Online Artifact,* and *Passage: Poems from the Landmark College Community.*

I am also very grateful to Landmark College for the gift of a sabbatical to work on this collection.

lie down too

Sex in the Farmyard by the Light of Mars

By the lights of cars and howling dogs, we attempt a mild form of honesty.

The afternoon slants in and cows stare out.

Your goal is to unload the trailer and mine is to fill the wood-shed.

We lie together in the sawdust.

Boulders will overflow our nests.

**To Give
Everything Away**

I dance and spray paint from my fingers.

I wear a pretty dress but curtsy clumsily.

I see broken glass no one else sees and then it is everywhere and I am in the hospital.

It is a bad time to get sick.

To get better, I need to give everything away.

Refrigerator Magnets

People are coming to visit us.

I cannot think of another way to start talking.

Preparations involve the refrigerator, a lime, and a bird.

The day that the word for the day was "friendly" is done.

Your mother marks you and you can paint her barn.

You can yell at me because I do everything wrong.

It would be beautiful if I were beautiful.

It's my heart I smoke.

I will know things later that if I knew now, they would change me and what I say.

We'll end up dead with a lot of notes about miracles.

The direction is a leaf to follow falling.

Every night it rains and she can't sleep.

To what kind of holy consciousness is ours so small?

Sugarloaf   The brightness of the day we descend from rapidly.

Wishing not to live longer but better, and alone in the wind, the afternoon, we stand looking out into the night past the names to the sea.

The wind won't settle.

The three points of a triangle move around.

Clocks go around with the world.

People keep calling our names.

They stare at other galaxies.

They age in one direction.

It happens all in one day.

We're not expecting anyone.

Nature is not wont to speak.

Our lives are not dictionaries.

One is drawing and one is color.

The background of the scene is in some unique proportion, one other than correct.

An old story of a house does not get told.

Our definitions run down a long straight road.

The stars fall into the ocean and we look at them as if they are only stars.

I walk into a shadow.

It occurs to me that without some confidence, it is difficult to work, and we must work.

At the Fountain in the Garden of the Asylum

Your trees are laden with huge branches of ripe nectarines and apricots.

Your hours are painted an unreal pink, your skies moony.

You said you enjoy being behind in your reading because the more you are behind the more you have to look forward to.

You are suffering an increased resiliency.

You go out to see Mars next to the moon. "It looks like Mars next to the moon," you say.

Oh, those baby eyes!

We put off discussion of the fountain because its centrality is formidable.

Long Division

I am dead, but to entertain and surprise everyone, I get up and dance.

I find myself spinning in a cow field.

I find myself alive at my teaching desk on Monday.

Animal parents love their children too.

I fall into a pitcher of milk.

I have big eyeholes.

The rubber band people come over for dinner.

We are no longer winners.

We are not competing.

We are feeling the sabi.

The gray and white cat between the mouse and the dog divides her attention.

You read ten haiku and in that time the woods get light.

Aretha and Giacometti

The mule stands just so to get that slice of morning glow.

You remove a horsefly from your coffee.

It's a short life so full of insects.

When you say, "Look at that," I look at the same time.

We never talk.

Impermanence at Hooper Dam

Heavy thoughts drift like weighing an elephant using a boat.

The inch of water deeper that the pond is than the dam goes over and over.

How will love be?

And how will you be?

How do we love and be angry, sisters and brothers?

Dust off your eyeballs and the infinite becomes three quarters of the picture.

Is a body of water a whole?

Its molecules go over the dam.

Cars go this way.

Cars go that.

We've been dropped on Earth.

Oh, a breeze.

Are we looking for a breeze?

Fear of Wolves

We are afraid of the wolves, and the dream is not the thing, and this is not Deer Park. When I leave you, I cannot worry about returning or if I will lose you. My skin is no divider between I would say myself and these trees, but no, there's no self. Sky and snow are the same color.

Can we open a book that breathes the same in as out? It's hard not to continue on a way that looks open. Because we could be even more fortunate, we feel not fortunate enough. We'll see what comes and who will have a biography. There was a moon. There was a murder.

Underneath, two formless things want to be together and they are both in a place they don't like, but neither will move and leave the other. Of course if one moves to a better place, the other will follow, or they could agree to move together.

We think of it as our path where we can fit between the trees. After our asylum, the mountain is a mountain again. Ice thaws and drips from an upper roof to a lower and then to the ground.

Please don't put your book between my book and my face. When number two is a reworking of number one, shouldn't we erase number one, so that there are not two things to deal with? We do away with pennies.

We have our talking-baby-dreams and then it's day, and we're fine and fine and sad and fine. We let our questions off their leashes and we head to the picture show lugging our philosophic backpacks. We walk, we run. Something else could happen.

The New One   Add one to one and it's always a new one: warm, dark, Delaware.

And every one can be divided: deck, Vienna, Virginia.

Lament   I'm running through a desert with my briefcase.

It's okay, this running, until it gets sadhearted.

I take to bed for a few years and the lament finally withers.

She becomes you.

All the possible combinations and not once did you consider her your dying companion.

In your heaven, she's not there.

My Sabbatical

I keep insects.

You can have one of my bees.

I breathe for you, bake for you, weep for you.

I'm right-handed and I like my coffee on my right.

You're like drawing from memory.

You're a bunch of leather-backed nonsense I'm in for.

I am not yearning so badly which doesn't mean I don't love you madly.

The Plastic Baby   You put the plastic baby on the moving walkway and took movies of its progress.

Is life so delicate?

Does it suffer?

You've left us wanting more, but not of this.

To stay with the accessible would be ridiculous.

The Nervous System is a Bird

The last time I saw you, you were still healthy and eating high fats. You were a religious bird believing in the consistency of your perceptions. You could fly on your own but chose the airlines.

I conceive of a nervous system apart from its body, a nervous system in a well-stocked library. Some connecting thread has been scissored so that the system can fly higher.

Red Bank

I wanted a horse.

I jumped from a plane.

I was not comfortable with your illness.

I was a detective at the wedding.

I recognized the new way it would be with you in rehabilitation.

I saw how the sunset colors on the Navesink River got sad with the lone rower.

I lived on a lone planet with my befuddlement.

I'd lost a person.

I didn't know how to hold my lips.

I was like the goose bathing in parking lot puddles.

Definitely, I am on a train.

February is a Hardworking Woman

Snow sits perfectly comfortably heavily on the wooden gate and red and silver chairs and iron table and the ornamental crabs.

We're expecting the spring return of tiny fellow eagernesses, but if retention of foliage through the winter may prove under such wet and heavy snow conditions to be something of a liability, then why be an evergreen or a false positive?

Every twig is so laden, every breath, every child so laden.

March Sun Grief   Temptation takes me to the river and gives me some good, good water. Then Doubt attacks; I let him is all. He says I won't live until spring, or I will, but someone I love won't. My work's an empty dodecahedron.

If you tell me my doubt is not religious, your lack of understanding is dark as a dark parking lot where I'm often waiting and if I'm not waiting there, I'm still waiting.

You know how the Ashuelot runs in the March sun? That's me; I'm ice on both sides and thawed in the middle. Faith-That-I'll-Make-It-To-April says I can touch her face; I'm guessing at this point that she's guessing too.

A yellow balloon drifts skyward in front of the Palisades Cliffs and she is gone—taking with her all my get-up-and-go, the way a container expands to hold the liquid that wants to be in it.

A small figure snowshoes a path. No one has a real name or golden chamber pot, but the figure is Mr. Richardson, plain-spoken. A mother mouse desperately moves her pinkies, who are also small New England experiences, to the shed. We burn the wood in the shed, and then we burn down the shed.

April Afternoons Our afternoons are either poet cats or girl poets. Once a month, they're adolescent girl cats modernistic. They catch moods with nets. They jump out of their minds, like fish out of pond water, for things to eat. They have zoom which doesn't mean there isn't obstacle after obstacle to their progressing. They are not good listeners. They thought we were saying the candy machine on the third floor was broken, but we were saying our girlfriends have left us and our hearts are broken. We beat our hearts. Coffee can only do so much but it does so much. Supposers sniff and run around our houses. We are melting off our ponds. We are baby woodpeckers.

If we sit in our boat in the cattails, it's a fact of temporality. A pair of mallards owns the pond and a pair of Canada geese and a pair of otters and a pair of tires and a thousand painted turtles. They're all at least a little mad at us. Our lessons don't seem to accumulate. We do six stanzas slowly and it is good for us. In our dayglow jewelry, we dance in the dark bathroom and it is a kind of happiness we are having.

**happy flags in
the fall**

If opposite things cannot exist at the same time, but only one after the other, then you can't sit on my bed while I'm in it.

The windows must be open morning and night.

Our thighs shut the doors.

We are floating in air, our feet higher than our heads.

We are one hundred percent here which is good before we have to leave.

We are odd together.

Two white chairs face each other.

The bridge is out, the one that connects any thought to any other.

We must drive a long ways around ourselves.

This is the most charming afternoon of the decade.

Flat Farm

The voices from a flat farm on a gray morn road—they are not used to having guests.

I wouldn't mind at all if they came down and made coffee.

If they, dear twenty-minute friends, only instead of barns of llamas had shops full of muffins and cakes, I would marry them!

Petronia Street

Artificial roses spill over from the Christian side.

Every dawn day here, we build up to sentences.

Is everything ready for language?

Everything is not.

I am surprised again and again by this arrowhead.

Instead of a pink taxi, you come to my gate in a pink flower.

**Between Love
and Departure**

A lemon tree in a pot on a deck near a fence near a pink wooden wall near a pool blows in a wind.

The line is not between art and compassion but between your own well-being and the less well-being of so many others.

Art is the path.

A rooster crows already, and the drunken crowds depart the streets.

Or between selfishness and compassion lies a pool of warm water.

Floating Journal   A fierce and brown rushing river does not wash you away, but this is how it happens.

You looked upstream to your history and down to your coming days and then you recognized your relative self, and upstream was your future and downstream your gone days.

Remission sometimes lasts long enough to feel like a true thing, a frog in a pond not eaten by a fish.

Your journal on a breakfast tray comes floating along.

lie down too

Only you are standing in the standing house.

You can't believe your sick insides don't show.

You take different slowdown pills.

The ocean in bed is calm and you will go there.

Four times now, you've been made younger with wanting to.

You dream you take a sleeping pill and sleep.

You look through the holiday ham to the bone and have visions.

It is sunny and flat and perfect.

Cows lie in the snow in the air direct from Labrador.

The sheep and the chair and the house lie down too.

April

You don't have the discipline to stand calm in all the quickly descending terraces of spring, but you know how to make vodka-ginger drinks and what to call them.

You don't want to work so hard and you don't want to not want to work so hard.

When a young woman breaks into song, you're not the only one crying.

You carry a sack. You disappear into your sack. Do you see yourself there?

I'll Laugh when I'm Ready

I'm sorry to keep leaving myself out, to forget to call your love over the mountains into a fog. I'm moving onto, and maturing into, confessing the first person who eats an orange and the orange is not real the way you know real. This leaves me alone again still not ready to laugh.

I'm floating with the rest of the pronouns, and first we come to turkeys and then cows and then their bones. It's one walk or another through the fields, through the towns, past the mill where it is raining. It's roofless; it's a puzzle. Lately I've been tortured by these abstractions when really they are only doors with knobs on the wrong side. I can't even break a single line without so much anxiety that I can't do it.

We sit outside at the tavern and eat and drink. It is a tiny complicated mess relieved by its name: worm. We drive home with an unhappy headache in the back seat. By ten o'clock, our glasses and our shoes and our sweaters have wandered off towards their own self-realizations. The terrific complexity of the moment is good enough. We fall asleep just as the animal wars begin.

My Last Day on Earth

I had a swift perception of relations: one road entering the village and one leaving.

While gazing at the clothesline towels, my squawking baby of a heart was growing.

This was my last day on Earth.

I was being imprisoned and then killed for my thoughts and still I thought them.

The roads I took were smaller and smaller.

There were fewer and fewer fellow travelers and fewer and fewer houses.

September Girl   She runs away.

When she goes home again, she gets punished.

She escapes again to the meadow where what was hard to cut close to is left to move back a few generations.

The shrubbery is left to stand and swaths mowed around every field.

September is the naked girl sitting on the abandoned farm machines.

Conscience and Gloom

A man does the same thing in many versions over and over.

He realizes art has no infinite shelf life.

His intelligence is a circle.

He is glad to be froglike and tender.

He is starting to depart.

The horizon is a line between life and death he throws himself over.

What's left is snow; depressions are daisies.

His chosen transportation is unreliable as the ice floes, the fountains, museums, and greenhouses of dreams.

Is he man, woman, or trouble?

He is conscience and gloom.

He is having a procedure on Wednesday.

He has been traveling.

He is standing frozen in the banks where they stop plowing Cook Hill Road.

The Russian Hunter

The Russian hunter feels a sudden tenderness towards the rabbit.

It knocks me over.

Tomorrow that will change, or anyway I will be surrounded by good intentions like a night full of stars, but saying anything beautifully belittles it by turning it into the beautiful saying and thereby forsaking its original nature.

My Darling Sabbatical, is it equal, what there is and what there isn't?

We will be young some spring morning.

And then a fetus in the sun.

Don't shuffle, old man!

Stand up straight, old woman!

Your time zone's not mine, but perhaps we share space.

We're all going to the same restaurant to have the same dinner.

Because nothing was not enough, did you say there is everything?

A calf has escaped, a house has burned, a man has died, a girl is born, someone buys a house, machines dig under the power lines.

The woods hardly get light through the shadows while backstage we have a drink.

Bear Questions   At the quarry floating, a big dead bear belly down.

What did he think before he died?

What if difficulty of access to the unconscious is its only defining feature?

We call Fish and Game and Fish and Game won't come.

Dreaming of a Meandering Proliferation of Leafy Vegetation

The eyes are bodies we twitch with.

For a bicycle, for a more musical life, we pine.

We are thinking on things to try and try and not even getting an ice cream.

We should travel upstream by train heading toward our futures and the future water.

We will be born in the city of elms.

We will know many famous elms.

Doomsday   The dog is hot enough to swim.

How lovely to have our own dog!

But if the poor dog wants in, we say sorry and keep her out.

If we are hungry, we are hot, and if we're stupid, we are eating bread.

We throw a dead-bloated-flyridden-maggoty cat off our driveway and across the road where we will forever after think of it being.

It's good to have nerve but nerves plural is an illness, a kind of doomsday weather.

The Sky is Overcast as My Head

We went to the gallery and then to get you a bike and then to sell a ring and then to drink tequila and then to watch a movie.

What a headache I have!

Where are my gold pills? My fake sky?

Our minds are shadows that hang over our hugely vague brains.

We build a long white bridge over the lake privately.

We don't need to talk about it (either).

It might as well (be) rain.

You drive away on your motorcycle and leave me all day.

There will be other afternoons, but never this storming one.

The sky is as overcast as my head.

There is no one to call.

The brain wants to run in its ruts.

Life Flying Away   You fight off feeling the suffering of others. You call your broken arm your army. You're King of the Third Floor. You can hear your food. You have a mood disorder. And a house and love disorder. We don't know what to do with you, and we have other worries too.

I want you to take off your pajamas. I want you to open a window for me. I want the back of your ear. I take a Polaroid of a Polaroid of a Polaroid of you at the city gates. Horses, cows, zebras, and giraffes graze within the city limits. Older citizens harvest what they can reach in the city orchards. The sooner we start over the better.

We leave a few girls and boys crying by the river. We commit strict and continuous self-examination. We try to take the friendly way in the shape of a walk that goes out, takes detours, wanders, and comes back a different way. Midnight and where are we? The house has opened itself, but we're not in it or even hovering by the back door smoking.

In a Big Modern House

A gentleman talks to his cat before talking to us about music in the lives of children.

Behind him a flock of gulls gathers, the clouds extra three dimensional and the ocean extra clean.

We ask, "What's the chance of six of any species being all male or all female and thereby unproductive?"

We put our hands on our knees.

Two knees, two hands!

We hang our identity papers out to dry in a springish breeze, and then we proceed without them.

Between the gentleman and the white roses, perfect sky and perfect skin, and counting halves instead of wholes, we've lost track of the breakfast eggs.

Questions of Faith

It's a thought experiment—how we do, how the world is written and how it is read. We smell cocaine and mist.

We try to knock the antlers off with a stick or kick them off, but they are firmly attached to the black and bloody mystery.

2.

In the mornings, our necks do not turn as easily.

We find peace in the windbent trees. She is a circle of sand and her lines are shells and coral and beach mud and beach pea leaves.

We have no fear of the lion's mouth from which we drink at the fountains in our peaceful courtyards.

3.

The sky's pink negative five. The ground's punctuated with holes from the snow spires of Fairy Valley City collapsed.

You say I punch and punch and you cannot breathe. Who am I to think you need to breathe faster?

4.

I snowshoe until I forget I am snowshoeing and just snowshoe, but to forget that I am living and live will never happen.

I am fortunate enough to hold the train of death's bride's dress.

A Wild Rushing Stream

The curtains of logic have fallen open.

All that's out here are more and more trees and different spaces between them.

If I go far enough, I find my bed to die in.

I have to walk away from Great Brook to rest my ears, to rest my nose from the water smell.

I am to return to the office of the woman who will say yes to my plans.

Geese return, buttons come undone, textiles relax.

I can become sick with muchness.

I can use the Shop-Vac, but I'm not saying that I have to.

Things are happening quickly.

We have a lot to organize in our heads.

The doctor will prescribe something quieter and warmer with cherry blossoms.

**Sick in the Rain
in Kolda**

I scare a stick-bed full of babies with my terrible white face.

I offer a village woman my teeth.

I hear pounding which is the sound of the endlessly multiplying outer circles of my not knowing, and also millet in the morning.

I grow a new pink fever orange which might be bad, or it might be good.

A Soiree at the Sanatorium

A mother is killed on the highway, her fawn hovering over her body. By philosophy's time we're counted broke.

My cat is a rolling prime number on hot brick. The bricks wobble, convalesce, and hallucinate. The sanatorium has theme and piano, a tour about, and special beverage experiments.

We pray for the gift of longer life sentences. On the continent behind the college, many boys and girls lie resting.

2.

We're good ninety percent of the time. We look work right in its dark eye.

The continent behind the college is spreading. It's not nonsense; it's Friday. An artist unhangs his show.

How the cracks between rocks and bricks fill with thyme, text and pots with sun, a television mutters, a mood shutters.

When you sit opposite from me at the café, I see what's behind you and you see what's behind me. Perhaps we should have been planning for this spontaneous conversation.

3.

Don't rush my sitting under the finch-book tree. It has been dark for ten days and like two eyes feed one brain, we go driving. We are on an expedition to see the big numbers and wreckage of the floods.

We are in a clock shop.

The End of Love   We kiss farewell like a final goodbye.

We're the very last of the Love People.

Old love junk washes up in the mangroves.

Spoo and Ta   Beginning with an *if*, we are oarless.

It's easy to run out of material and fall back on wide gray boards.

Sometimes it's no duality, but more a spoked wheel November rolls in on.

The leaves on the trees cry, "Mercy on us who feel all pain and woozy."

You had a crash—next thing you know, a shot of morphine. Morphine has no hair, no book, no man, and no money. Can she be redirected? You are lying on the floor near the door. Everything you own is dripped with paint. The fan turning could cut off your fingers. It has your thinking. You feel a decrease in hunger. It's a drift off of your central nervous system like a horizon line stick figures dance on. It's easy being chipper in your house with its open windows, flowers, and paintings, but what about your Bob? You'll eat soon and have a little book with your food.

2.

I'm sorry; did I cut you off? There are many Manchesters, many writers of the same book, many seekers that have come down.

The Skeleton Inside the Flesh of the Young Woman Reclining

Under the table in your living room in a box you've never seen before, sits a perfect country house.

Make yourself a bower, put thee a statue and another vow not to whimper.

No one calls on you to do anything brave.

You have a new sweater.

Sometimes you are given enough to eat and sometimes not.

Are you saying you'll never be so carefree as to build a folly in the gardens?

A temple of modern or ancient virtue in ruins?

An atmosphere of fruitful melancholy?

It's not that you don't want to be of service.

Oh, the Fun it was Fishing in the Back Country!

They wave their arms slowly and sway. They've taken another step closer to stepping away from the flat earth but they can't completely give up being professional people. On their asymmetric island, two are only two and not yet a pattern. "We aren't yet a pattern," said two of them. Is there not a horse or a cow on the whole island?

In the medicine garden, Humble Bob leads them to revelation. They take the roosters, scooters, and girls along, the boating people, the fishing people, the drinking people, the writing people, the shopping people, all those fish-eaters. They roll up their pants and clown around. One family takes their suitcases and rolls them across the courtyard and through the gatehouse to wait in the lane for a taxi to take them to the airport where they will catch their first plane for the journey north to home. And the big imagination cruise ship takes up the whole horizon, then sails away.

No one asks for my ideas, but I have lots of ideas. They circle around. They bike around the cemetery enough at night and they get turned around. They think they see goats there.

A Ferryboat Ride   They think it impossible to live with such watery awareness.

By morning the thought is banished and the ferryboat takes them back to the mainland.

How quickly there is great water between them and the island!

"It's a flag-waving perfect weather day for a ferryboat ride," they say.

They know that all is well not because it ends that way but because it is that way now.

These Appointed Rounds

Neither snow nor rain will stop them.

Nor a broken gutter fountain.

Nor will heat stop them.

Nor will the gloom of night where we want to show them our secret stash.

Nothing stays these couriers, but some recognition of themselves in ourselves.

The city is abuzz with their generosity.

Down below the buildings the sun hardly stabs them.

August　　　　We float face up.

When we look back, there's no ahead.

The tops of trees, the mommies and girls, are in the sky.

We regain our momentum and desire.

We're mostly brain and the house is full of sleepers still.

The frogs think we are weeds.

We're in the mood and going down.

Nude

We read slowly our days and more quickly the nights and we dream them not to remember.

The sea-rock nude lies down.

Her outlines wrap like the wind, like gin, like grass and sand.

Her causes are so many knotted ropes of wild speculation.

We'll run out of days before we reach the spot where she dances by the metrical sea.

The Abstractionist

Tell the abstractionist what you want her to tell you, but it's a bad idea to tell her good friends break up over ideas.

She's your good friend and she's helpless.

She's been sorrowfully awed by your inability to draw and your resistance to both abstractions and medications when the bodily world is insufficient.

The earth hangs and the abstractionist hangs on to it.

Her life and her thinking are twins and it's the nature of their twinhood to compete and to love each other terribly, to need each other endlessly.

I See My Categories Have Been All Wrong up Until Now

You enter the philosopher's gallery.

Your categories have been all wrong up until now.

No adjective is small enough for the work you do in your life on the planet.

Are you trying to be me sleeping on my side of the bed after all these years?

The Moon	There is no tarred black road and nobody is walking on it.

I think I understand and what I understand is tiring.

I understand your discomforts discomfort me.

A vehicle, a white delivery truck, makes its way.

A bull is crashing his horns into the brushpile.

Christmas Lights   We walk down an alley of birches.

For protection against the ridiculous, we take suitcases full of books.

We learn that when the time comes to say as truthfully as we can all that we think we know, the sky really falls.

Life is a moment of chickens and then one chicken.

Everyone is excited about the storms and the wars.

They're saying snow at dawn.

No one is able to get to church.

The man hangs himself in his dreams.

**The Happiest
Girl**

Like these hours before dinner if she's not drinking, the air
between them is visible. She wants to sleep without deciding
to, without going to. Her desire becomes the fuel for invention
or the layer of sympathy she lays over everything or a state of
permanent agitation that she's come to consider what life really
is. She thinks sometimes she is the happiest girl.

2.

Hills blend with indoor reflections, then diminish, then are
replaced by doors like passing clouds the color of fog. It doesn't
matter if she rushes or meanders within her ten-foot square.
The color of the boy dripping by the pool is white. The monkeys
of North Adams, are they mad or mystical?

By the River   In our college years, we watched the Hudson flow.

We bathed in extravagant fountains in abandoned formal gardens.

By taxis we went to the drinking hole, Home of Suffering in Art, and we lay on the couches in that home.

Napping has since become our spiritual practice.

We sleep by the Connecticut.

How flat the water tries to be!

The fog has flowed with the water south.

I think it is good to leave civilization slowly.

Book Benefactors

Alice James Books and Lesle Lewis wish to thank the following individuals, who generously contributed toward the publication of *lie down too*:

> *Anonymous*
> *Kazim Ali*
> *Nancy Lagomarsino*

For more information about AJB's book benefactor program, contact us via phone or email, or visit us at www.alicejamesbooks.org to see a list of forthcoming titles.

Recent Titles from Alice James Books

Panic, Laura McCullough
Milk Dress, Nicole Cooley
Parable of Hide and Seek, Chad Sweeney
Shahid Reads His Own Palm, Reginald Dwayne Betts
How to Catch a Falling Knife, Daniel Johnson
Phantom Noise, Brian Turner
Father Dirt, Mihaela Moscaliuc
Pageant, Joanna Fuhrman
The Bitter Withy, Donald Revell
Winter Tenor, Kevin Goodan
Slamming Open the Door, Kathleen Sheeder Bonanno
Rough Cradle, Betsy Sholl
Shelter, Carey Salerno
The Next Country, Idra Novey
Begin Anywhere, Frank Giampietro
The Usable Field, Jane Mead
King Baby, Lia Purpura
The Temple Gate Called Beautiful, David Kirby
Door to a Noisy Room, Peter Waldor
Beloved Idea, Ann Killough
The World in Place of Itself, Bill Rasmovicz
Equivocal, Julie Carr
A Thief of Strings, Donald Revell
Take What You Want, Henrietta Goodman

Alice James Books has been publishing poetry since 1973 and remains one of the few presses in the country that is run collectively. The cooperative selects manuscripts for publication primarily through regional and national annual competitions. Authors who win a Kinereth Gensler Award become active members of the cooperative board and participate in the editorial decisions of the press. The press, which historically has placed an emphasis on publishing women poets, was named for Alice James, sister of William and Henry, whose fine journal and gift for writing went unrecognized during her lifetime.

TYPESET AND DESIGNED BY MIKE BURTON

PRINTED BY KASE PRINTING

ON SFI CERTIFIED, ACID FREE PAPER